REAL-LIFE
SCIENTIFIC
ADVENTURES

ROALD AMUNDSEN REACHES THE SOUTH POLE

RACHAEL MORLOCK

PowerKiDS
press™

New York

Published in 2019 by The Rosen Publishing Group, Inc.
29 East 21st Street, New York, NY 10010

First Edition

Editor: Theresa Morlock
Book Design: Reann Nye

Photo Credits: Cover, pp. 1 UniversalImagesGroup/Universal Images Group/Getty Images; p. 4 Li Hui Chen/Shutterstock.com; pp. 5, 9 (top) Rainer Lesniewski/Shutterstock.com; p. 6 Exclusive Aerials/Shutterstock.com; p. 7 Courtesy of the National Library of Norway/Wikimedia Commons; p. 9 (bottom) Hulton Archive/Getty Images; p. 11 (top) Photo 12/Universal Images Group/Getty Images; pp. 11 (bottom), 15 (both), 16, 19, 22, 29 Courtesy of the National Library of Norway Flickr; p. 12 Sean M Smith/Shutterstock.com; p. 13 (top) Peter & J Clement/Science Source/Getty Images; p. 13 (bottom) AndreAnita/Shutterstock.com; pp. 17 Hulton Deutsch/Corbis Historical/Getty Images; p. 21 (top) Bettmann/Getty Images pp. 21 (bottom), 26 Hulton Deutsch/Corbis Historical/Getty Images; p. 23 (top) https://commons.wikimedia.org/wiki/File:Teltleir_med_sleder_hunder_og_annet_utstyr,_1911_(7675743094).jpg; p. 23 (bottom) https://commons.wikimedia.org/wiki/File:Ekspedisjon_med_sleder_og_hundespann,_1911-1912_(12114495993).jpg; p. 24 Yevgen Belich/Shutterstock.com; p. 25 (top) Evikka/Shutterstock.com; p. 25 (bottom) Danita Delimont/ Gallo Images/Getty Images; p. 27 (top) https://commons.wikimedia.org/wiki/File:H._R._Bowers,_Terra_Nova_expedition_at_the_South_Pole,_1912.png; p. 27 (bottom) https://en.wikipedia.org/wiki/Robert_Falcon_Scott#/media/File:Cross_on_Observation_Hill,_McMurdo_Station.jpg; p. 28 Keystone/Hulton Archive/Getty Images.

Cataloging-in-Publication Data

Names: Morlock, Rachael.
Title: Roald Amundsen reaches the south pole / Rachael Morlock.
Description: New York : PowerKids Press, 2019. | Series: Real-life scientific adventures | Includes glossary and index.
Identifiers: LCCN ISBN 9781508168607 (pbk.) | ISBN 9781508168584 (library bound) | ISBN 9781508168614 (6 pack)
Subjects: LCSH: Amundsen, Roald, 1872-1928–Juvenile literature. | Explorers–Norway–Biography–Juvenile literature. | South Pole–Discovery and exploration–Juvenile literature.
Classification: LCC G585.A6 M68 2019 | DDC 919.89–dc23

Manufactured in the United States of America

CPSIA Compliance Information: Batch #CS18PK: For Further Information contact Rosen Publishing, New York, New York at 1-800-237-9932

CONTENTS

ANTARCTICA

For many years, people believed there must be a land at the bottom of the world. It wasn't until 1820 that someone sailed far enough south to see the **mainland** of Antarctica. It would take decades before anyone could reach it and explore. When they did, they found a large, windy continent of ice and snow.

Antarctica has an unfriendly climate. About 99 percent of the land is covered in ice. It's too cold and dark for trees to grow. Only a few types of animals, such as penguins and seals, can survive along its coasts. Despite Antarctica's challenges, many adventurers and scientists of the 1800s and 1900s were excited to go there. It was one of the last places in the world that hadn't been explored and **documented**.

Sea ice surrounding the mainland makes it difficult for ships to reach Antarctica. The actual shape and size of the continent were unknown for many years.

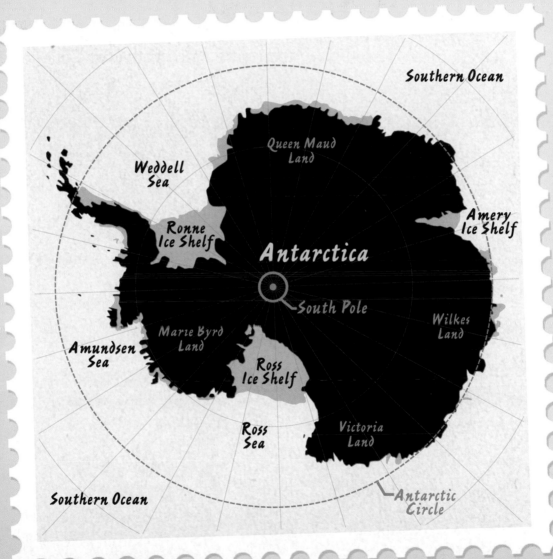

Southern Ocean

Weddell Sea

Queen Maud Land

Amery Ice Shelf

Ronne Ice Shelf

Antarctica

South Pole

Wilkes Land

Amundsen Sea

Marie Byrd Land

Ross Ice Shelf

Ross Sea

Victoria Land

Antarctic Circle

Southern Ocean

AMUNDSEN THE EXPLORER

Roald Amundsen was determined to discover the secrets of the Arctic and Antarctic regions. Even as a 15-year-old, Amundsen dreamed of becoming an explorer. He read as much as he could about journeys near the North and South Poles. Growing up in Norway, he practiced skiing, mountain climbing, and **navigating** snowy landscapes. He slept with his windows open during winter nights to build up his strength in cold weather.

EXPEDITION REPORT

The Northwest Passage is an Arctic waterway between the Atlantic and Pacific Oceans. To safely make the trip, Amundsen followed the example of native Arctic people by wearing furs and using a small boat. He led the first expedition to sail through the Northwest Passage.

In 1897, Amundsen joined his first expedition to Antarctica on board the *Belgica*. He learned from the mistakes and successes of the journey. In 1903, Amundsen made history as captain of an important Arctic expedition through the Northwest Passage. When he returned, he began planning again. He wanted to be the first person to reach the North Pole.

RACE TO THE POLE

Amundsen's plans changed when American explorer Robert Peary made headlines around the world. He reported reaching the North Pole on April 6, 1909. Amundsen already had a ship and polar gear, but now his goal shifted. If he couldn't be first to reach the North Pole, then he would try for the South Pole.

The British explorer Robert Falcon Scott was already planning a scientific exploration of Antarctica and a trip to the South Pole. Amundsen would have to compete with Scott. He decided to keep his goal a secret. He set sail from Norway in early June 1910. When the expedition reached its first landing, Amundsen revealed his plan. Instead of traveling around South America and continuing north, they would sail to Antarctica.

EXPEDITION REPORT

As Earth travels around the sun, it spins on an imaginary axis, or pole. This pole runs through the center of the planet, from north to south. The north end is in the Arctic, and the south end is in Antarctica.

South Pole

Amundsen's journey — Scott's journey

Marie Byrd
Land

Ross
Ice Shelf

Victoria
Land

Bay of
Whales

Ross
Island

Ross Sea

Amundsen sent a
telegram to tell Scott
his plans. He would
land in a different
area than Scott and
make his own route
to the South Pole.

Robert Falcon Scott

PLANNING AND PREPARING

Before leaving Norway, Amundsen spent time in **detailed** and thoughtful planning. He based his preparations on other journeys. Amundsen knew that staying warm, eating well, and traveling quickly would be key to survival and success.

Native people in the Arctic had taught him the best way to wear reindeer skins. With skins, wool, and sturdy boots, the expedition members could stay warm and dry in the freezing temperatures. Amundsen also knew the importance of healthy food. His crew would eat fresh seal meat to prevent **scurvy**.

During his time in the Arctic, Amundsen had learned the value of dogs. They could handle low temperatures, scramble up mountainsides, and pull **sledges** through deep snow. He chose teams of dogs for carrying supplies to the pole.

EXPEDITION REPORT

A surprising member of the Fram's crew was a canary named Fridtjof. The bird traveled from Norway to Antarctica, then sailed with the ship from South America to Africa and back. Fridtjof was probably the first feathered polar explorer.

Amundsen's expedition set sail on the *Fram*. This ship belonged to the Norwegian explorer Fridtjof Nansen. It was specially built for sailing through icy waters.

Amundsen and his dog sled team

THE ROSS ICE SHELF

The *Fram* sailed into the Bay of Whales on January 14, 1911. December and January are among the warmest months in Antarctica. Higher temperatures allow ships to reach the continent with less risk of becoming trapped in ice. Amundsen chose this spot on the Ross Ice Shelf for landing. He would make camp on the large bar of ice.

McMurdo Sound

Scott and his crew landed at McMurdo Sound, also on the enormous Ross Ice Shelf. Scott had been there before. He would use a route he had followed partway in an earlier attempt to reach the pole. Amundsen's trip would begin 69 miles (111 km) closer to their goal, but it would cross unknown land. Both groups prepared for the long, dark winter on the ice.

At the Bay of Whales, the *Fram's* crew divided into two groups. One set sail again to record **oceanographic** information. The other prepared for the South Pole trip.

13

WINTER AT FRAMHEIM

Before the winter weather began, Amundsen and his team set up depots on the way to the pole. Depots are storage areas for food and supplies. The team placed 7,500 pounds (3,401.9 kg) of goods along the route south. The depots would allow them to renew their supplies as they traveled. They would have enough **materials** to reach the pole without overloading their sleds.

After their depot trips, the Norwegians returned to camp. They had built a winter base about 2.5 miles (4 km) from the sea. It was named Framheim after their ship. In addition to a wooden hut, the base had tunnels cut into the ice. These led to storage areas, workspaces, and a **sauna** large enough for one person.

EXPEDITION REPORT

Antarctic temperatures are usually below freezing. Winter temperatures have dropped as low as -129°F (-89°C)! There are two seasons—six months of winter darkness and six months of summer daylight. At the South Pole, there's one sunrise and one sunset a year.

There was plenty to do at Framheim. The team prepared supplies and trained their dogs. Depot trips were test runs that helped the crew perfect their gear and plans.

The interior of Framheim

TO THE POLE!

Amundsen's crew worked throughout the long, dark winter. They made their sledges lighter, prepared their gear, and packed supplies so they would be ready when the daylight and warmer weather came. In September, the polar party left Framheim. However, their first night on the ice proved that the weather wasn't warm enough for the dogs. In the morning, the dogs were too stiff to stand up on their own. Amundsen realized the expedition would have to wait a little longer.

EXPEDITION REPORT

At Framheim, the men cooked pancakes, bread, and seal and penguin meat. They ate more simply on the ice. Biscuits, powdered milk, chocolate, and frozen seal meat provided energy. The men and dogs also ate pemmican, a mix of crushed, dried meat.

Amundsen's expedition traveled for five or six hours a day across the Ross Ice Shelf. The men gave the dogs a break every hour so they wouldn't be too worn out.

The expedition set out again on October 19, 1911. The men traveled on skis while 52 dogs pulled the sledges. The men were all natural and skilled skiers. They moved quickly across the ice shelf and avoided unsafe crevasses, or gaps, in the ice and snow.

CROSSING THE MOUNTAINS

On November 17, 1911, Amundsen's group arrived at the Transantarctic Mountains. They made a depot at the base of the mountains to lighten their load. Amundsen named a glacier ahead of them "Axel Heiberg," after one of the expedition's supporters. To continue, they had to climb the steep, snowy, and icy glaciers.

The polar **plateau** lay on the other side of the mountains. This was a stretch of land with even snow for the sledges, and they traveled quickly. The wind roared and temperatures dropped as they moved south. Despite their warm gear, some of the men suffered from frostbite. This harmful condition occurs when body parts become too cold. The dogs also grew cold, tired, and hungry. Some dogs were killed to feed the others.

Crossing the Axel Heiberg glacier was a difficult feat. The men and dogs climbed **10,000** feet **(3,048 m)** and traveled **44** miles **(70.8 km)** to pass the Transantarctic Mountains.

AT THE SOUTH POLE

Amundsen made careful **geographic** observations and used special tools to keep track of their location. The group reached the geographic South Pole on December 14, 1911. No human had ever been there before. There was nothing to mark this as the farthest point south in the world. Only Amundsen's observations could show that he had at last reached the South Pole!

Together, Amundsen's crew planted a Norwegian flag in the snow. They set up a tent in a place they named "Polheim." Amundsen worried they might be mistaken in their navigation. To be sure that Norwegians stood at the actual South Pole, he sent his men out in different directions to circle the area. After three days near the South Pole, the crew left to begin the return journey.

Amundsen checked and double-checked his readings using navigating
tools. A tool called a sextant was used for finding latitude and
longitude and compasses gave information about direction.

THE RACE CONTINUES

Before leaving Polheim, Amundsen wrote letters to Scott and the king of Norway. He left them in the tent along with a few spare supplies. If Amundsen didn't survive, then at least Scott would know of his success.

It was clear that Amundsen had beaten Scott to the South Pole, but the race wasn't over yet. In addition to being first to the South Pole, Amundsen also wanted to be first to announce his victory. If Amundsen didn't move quickly, Scott might still beat him in sharing the news with the world. Fortunately, sunny, calm weather was on the group's side. Thanks to his careful planning, Amundsen's team also had plenty of food, supplies, and rest. They made a swift return to Framheim.

Skis and well-trained dogs allowed Amundsen's crew to travel very quickly. They covered about 15 to 30 miles (24.1 to 48.3 km) a day on their way back from the South Pole.

A HEROIC JOURNEY

Amundsen returned to Framheim on January 25, 1912. His entire polar journey had lasted for 99 days and covered 1,860 miles (2,993.4 km) of unmapped territory. Every member of his crew survived and returned in good health. Amundsen's detailed planning had led to a brilliantly successful expedition. A few days later, Amundsen boarded the *Fram* and sailed off to share his news with the world.

The *Fram* landed in Hobart, Tasmania, on March 7, 1912. Amundsen sent telegrams about his exciting achievement to his brother Leon, to the

Hobart, Tasmania

Norwegian king, and to Fridtjof Nansen. He wrote the telegrams in a secret code. Very soon, the news spread around the globe. People had reached the South Pole—one of the last unexplored places on Earth!

The Norwegian South Pole explorers are honored at a museum in Oslo, Norway. Statues represent the five members of the polar expedition: Olav Bjaaland, Oscar Wisting, Roald Amundsen, Sverre Hassel, and Helmer Hanssen.

Roald Amundsen statue at Polar Museum, Tromso, Norway

SCOTT'S FATE

The pride and sense of achievement Amundsen took in his expedition soon faded. On February 10, 1913, terrible news about Scott's expedition cast a shadow over Amundsen's success.

Scott and his team had arrived at the South Pole and the tent at Polheim on January

Robert Falcon Scott

17, 1912. By the time they reached the pole, Scott's men were already tired and weak. The ponies they had chosen weren't suited to the climate and died. Without them, the crew made slow progress. They suffered through frostbite, hunger, and blizzards. All five members of Scott's expedition died during their return from the South Pole. Scott recorded the story of their suffering and courage in his journal. He made his last entry on March 29, 1912.

A search party later found the bodies of Scott and two of his men. Their records, including Scott's final message and this photo from the South Pole, told their sad tale.

The Observation Hill cross was erected in 1913 as a memorial to Scott and his party.

AMUNDSEN'S ADVENTURES

Amundsen had reached the South Pole, but he wasn't finished. He used the skills that made his South Pole expedition a success and began planning new adventures. Since he'd already traveled through the Northwest Passage, he next sailed through the Northeast Passage.

In 1926, he led the first expedition to fly over the North Pole. Oscar Wisting, part of his South Pole team, joined him. Amundsen and Wisting were the first people to cross both the North and South Poles.

Amundsen and his airplane went missing on June 18, 1928, during a rescue mission over the Arctic. He left behind the inspiring stories of his explorations. With bravery, a thirst for adventure, and careful planning, Amundsen opened the door to some of the world's most secret and challenging places.

Amundsen led the way south with great courage, planning, and skill. Another 40 years passed before another explorer, Sir Edmund Hillary, successfully journeyed to and from the South Pole on land.

Amundsen's Adventures

December 31, 1902
Ernest Shackleton, Edward Wilson, and Robert Falcon Scott give up their goal of reaching the South Pole on the Discovery Expedition.

June 16, 1903–August 31, 1906
Roald Amundsen leads the first successful sea journey through the Northwest Passage.

January 9, 1909
Shackleton's Nimrod Expedition comes within about 100 miles (160.9 km) of the South Pole but is forced to turn back.

April 6, 1909
Robert Peary reportedly reaches the North Pole. His claim, however, may not be true.

June 1910
Amundsen and the *Fram* set sail for Antarctica.

June 15, 1910
Scott and the *Terra Nova* set sail for Antarctica.

January 14, 1911
Amundsen and the *Fram* land at the Ross Ice Shelf.

October 19, 1911
Amundsen leaves Framheim to find the South Pole.

December 14, 1911
Amundsen and four of his men reach the South Pole.

January 17, 1912
Scott's party reaches the South Pole.

January 25, 1912
Amundsen and his polar party return to the *Fram*.

January 30, 1912
The *Fram* sets sail from Antarctica.

March 7, 1912
Amundsen, his crew, and the *Fram* arrive in Tasmania and announce their victory.

March 29, 1912
Scott makes his final diary entry.

June 18, 1928
Amundsen goes missing during a rescue mission in the Arctic Sea.

December 14, 1928
South Pole Day is declared in Norway to honor Amundsen.

GLOSSARY

detailed: Having many details, or small parts or features.

document: To study and record.

geographic: Of or relating to geography, or the science that deals with the Earth and its life.

mainland: The main part of a continent, not the islands surrounding it.

material: Something from which something else can be made.

navigate: To find one's way.

oceanographic: Of or relatings to oceanography, or the science that deals with the ocean.

plateau: A broad, flat, raised area of land.

sauna: A steam bath.

scurvy: A disease caused by lack of vitamin C.

sledge: A vehicle on runners for carrying loads or passengers over snow or ice.

INDEX

WEBSITES

Due to the changing nature of Internet links, PowerKids Press has developed an online list of websites related to the subject of this book. This site is updated regularly. Please use this link to access the list: www.powerkidslinks.com/rlsa/roald